US NAVAL
AIRPOWER

Supercarrier in action

Photography by Neil Leifer
Text by Bill Sweetman

Motorbooks International
Publishers & Wholesalers Inc
Osceola Wisconsin 54020 USA

First published in 1987 by Motorbooks International Publishers & Wholesalers Inc, PO Box 2, 729 Prospect Avenue, Osceola, WI 54020 USA

Motorbooks International is a certified trademark, registered with the United States Patent Office

Printed and bound in Hong Kong

The information in this book is true and complete to the best of our knowledge. All recommendations are made without any guarantee on the part of the author or publisher, who also disclaim any liability incurred in connection with the use of this data or specific details

Library of Congress
  Cataloging-in-Publication Data
ISBN 0-87938-246-5

Motorbooks International books are also available at discounts in bulk quantity for industrial or sales-promotional use. For details write to Special Sales Manager at the Publisher's address

On the front cover: Wedge-shaped external compression inlets feed the F-14's Pratt & Whitney TF30-P-412A augmented turbofans, and make it one of the two fastest US fighters. The engine, however, is part of the F-14A's basic problems. The aircraft was designed in 1968 as a substitute for the F-111B, a naval version of the USAF's F-111 which had proved to be too heavy for carrier operations. To cut development time and cost, the Navy decided to fit the engines and fire-control system of the F-111B in the first examples of the new fighter, installing more powerful engines from ship number 64 and later updating the electronics. The best laid plans.. . . Cost overruns and budget cuts destroyed the plan and all the F-14s built to date have been the "interim" F-14A model. Now, however, two new versions are under development: the F-14A Plus, with the more powerful and far better handling General Electric F110 engine; and the F-14D, with the new engine and a completely new avoinics suite.

On the back cover: Any military pilot will tell you that carrier flying takes special qualities. It is probably the most hazardous and certainly the most stressful flying job short of actual combat. Pilots like this SLUF driver in an A-7E make their living by bringing their aircraft, day after day, onto a heaving, pitching, rolling patch of steel in the open ocean.

On the frontispiece: Long-range interceptor, short-range dogfighter and movie star, the dramatically sculpted Grumman F-14A Tomcat is the fleet's first defense line. Advanced aerodynamic design, heavyweight missiles and sophisticated avionics put it among the world's top fighters. USS *Carl Vinson* numbers twenty-four Tomcats in its eighty-six-plane air force.

On the title page: A carrier is not only big, but it must be fast in order to launch aircraft in a flat calm, and maneuverable so that her turns into the wind to launch aircraft do not consume too much time. Among the US Navy's supercarriers, *Nimitz*, *Vinson*, *Enterprise* and the new ships now being built are nuclear powered. One of the advantages of nuclear power for a carrier is that high speeds can be sustained without worrying about fuel supplies. Transit or regular cruising speeds, however, are lower than the Navy expected. They are not limited by fuel or power, but by the fact that mechanical and hydrodynamic noise at high speed deafens the fleet to the sound of submarines.

On this page: The island juts from the deck like a futurist office block, incorporating the captain's bridge, lookout station and Pri-Fly. Apart from the control of aircraft on the deck, the island is mainly used for peacetime navigation. Modern naval warfare is almost invariably fought beyond visual range; indeed, if an adversary is within sight of the *Vinson*'s island in wartime, something has probably gone wrong. The island also carries the ship's own radars—used sparingly or, during an emissions control (EMCON) exercise, not at all—and its own electronic countermeasures (ECM) equipment.

Contents

USS *Carl Vinson:*
carrier, command, crew

"Aircraft carrier" is a literal and unpoetic term for the world's largest warships. The aircraft carrier is many things apart from a ship. It is a floating airbase, a symbol of power and a seagoing home to more than 5,000 men. In fact, the crew complement of a carrier is three times that of the biggest battleship of the 1940s. Every member of the crew, from the captain and the commander of the air wing to the first-cruise enlisted man, is trained in and works in the culture of naval aviation, a culture that addresses the demands of survival in the world's two most unforgiving professions: seamanship and aviation. Watching some of the inhabitants of this small city gives some idea of the challenges they routinely face in their day-to-day work.

An aircraft carrier is an offensive weapon. US Navy doctrine states that, in the event of war with the Soviet Union, the USS *Carl Vinson* and its escorts, as part of the Pacific fleet, will steam toward the Soviet Navy's eastern strongholds between Kamchatka and Vladivostok. They will close the narrow seas between these bases and the Pacific, to prevent Soviet surface vessels and submarines from closing the West's arterial sealanes, and launch intensive day and night airstrikes against Soviet ships, airfields and shore facilities. Captain Thomas Mercer is responsible for ensuring that his ship will be ready to carry out such a raid and survive.

Where is the engine-room telegraph, dammit? A fleece-covered armchair and a computer terminal may seem more appropriate to Wall Street than to the bridge of the US Navy's newest and heaviest carrier, but information counts for much more to the men aboard the *Vinson* than it does to the hottest brokerage firm. The real command post on the ship, from which Captain Mercer and his officers would manage a battle against enemies far beyond visual range, is correctly called the Combat Information Center (CIC). It is many feet below the bridge, buried inside the ship for protection against a blast and nuclear, biological and chemical weapons. For now, the ship is not on alert, Mercer can occupy the captain's traditional place on the bridge, and the computer terminals are his link to the CIC.

Officially, he is the Air Operations Officer, and unofficially, the Air Boss. As long as his watch lasts, he is undisputed ruler of the *Vinson*'s six-acre deck and the sky immediately around it. With the skill of a choreographer, the Air Boss plots the intricate dance of airplanes, support carts and men on the flight deck, so that aircraft are launched in the fastest possible sequence and nobody has to hang around the sky, waiting for the rest of the formation and burning fuel. The Air Boss sets the order in which thirsty airplanes and tired pilots will be recovered to the carrier, and is responsible for traffic patterns around the ship. His throne is Pri-Fly, perched atop the carrier's "island," the massive steel office block that juts from the deck. He has a full view of three quarters of a circle to command the entire space of the deck.

Next page
Ready rooms are on the O-3 level, above the hangars and below the flight deck, for the simple reason that flying a carrier mission is hard enough work without having to run up six flights of stairs, in full flying kit and a heavy seaway, in order to reach your aircraft. Each squadron has its own ready room, so that several different missions to be launched in the same cycle can be briefed simultaneously, but the result is that the ready rooms—like every other space on the *Vinson*—are not overlarge.

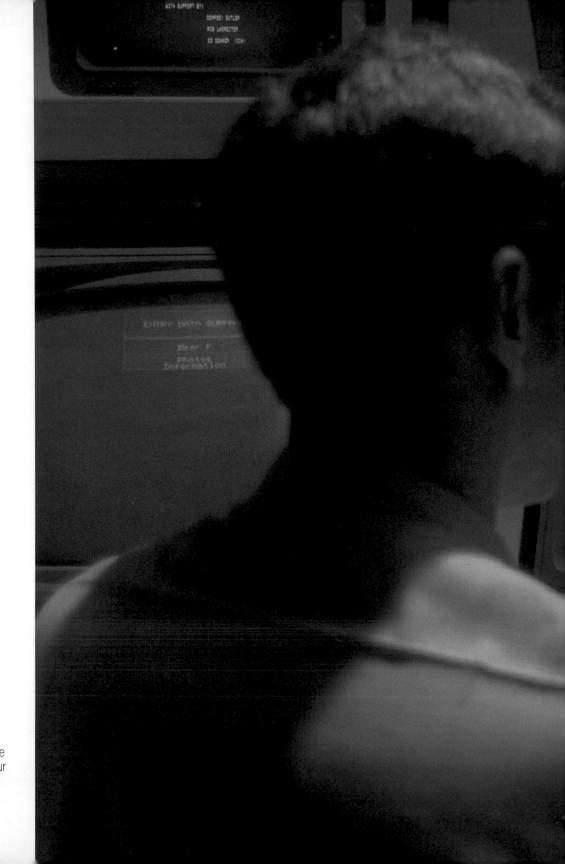

Intelligence on air and missile threats is part of
every briefing, and like any sizable base, the
Vinson carries its own intelligence officers. A
computerized database, menu-driven, allows the
Vinson's crew to update themselves on the latest
trends in the threat. A three-view drawing, though,
is hardly necessary to identify the Soviet Navy's
Tupolev Tu-142 Bear bomber and reconnaissance
aircraft, shown here. The 190 ton Bear, with its four
15,000 horsepower turboprop engines, has an
almost unbelievable range, and tracks carrier
groups far out into the open ocean.

While Pri-Fly is the carrier's control tower, most of the air traffic around the ship is well beyond visual range, just as it is around any air base, and most of the air traffic control task is handled by operators in darkened rooms. Here, in the Carrier Air Traffic Control Center (CATCC), controllers monitor which flights have been launched, which are due to be launched, and which are due for recovery. Instead of a radar scope, their most important tool is a range of perspex panels that show which crews and aircraft are airborne, which are scheduled to launch and when each is expected to return. Air refueling is also controlled from here.

Next page

A simple and reliable large-format display, used in several places on the ship, is a perspex screen on which an enlisted man writes backward in a contrasting colored crayon. Careful lighting ensures that the letters are readable. This display, on the bridge, shows the maneuver history and planned maneuvers of the carrier and its escorts.

The carrier deck and the hangar deck are small spaces when one considers that dozens of large aircraft must be moved on time and in sequence to elevators and catapults, that maintenance people must have room to work around them, and that space must be left on deck for launch and recovery. Here, a crewman uses a reliable, nonelectronic means to solve a complex puzzle, with two-dimensional models, each representing the area or "spot" occupied by an aircraft. "Spot factor" is an important element in naval aircraft design; note how even the big F-14s, in the top right-hand corner of the model, can be packed densely with their wings swept back.

Working in red light behind their perspex display screens, enlisted men in the CATCC are barely visible as they update information on the operations of the carrier's air wing. The task is complicated; some operations, such as airstrikes, are out-and-return missions while other activities, such as maintaining the defensive fighter and antisubmarine screens, continue around the clock. Emergencies or precautionary landings can disrupt the whole picture, so that, more so than in most traffic control centers, the CATCC is a place where quick decisions are made. Radar is available, and is visible in front of the controller on the right, but cannot be freely used because it betrays the ship's track and position; for that reason, the perspex display screens are given more prominence.

Previous page
The catapult watch booth, a cubicle half-sunk into the deck with narrow windows like an armored truck's, is home to the catapult operator. His job is to make sure that the catapult is functioning correctly and, on a signal from the catapult operator on the deck, to fire the waiting aircraft off the end of the ship. After the catapult operator punches the button, it's all up to the crew, the engines and Sir Isaac Newton.

Off southern California, close to Catalina and San Clemente Islands, an enlisted man prepares a map to guide the CATCC controllers through a series of bombing exercises. Commercial flight lanes between Los Angeles and Hawaii must be carefully avoided. The centroid of the map's circular grid is on the approximate position of the carrier, but the map points out one of the unique features of carrier traffic control: The traffic control center and the "airfield" itself are constantly moving and can change course in any direction at any time.

A respite from activity, with no recoveries expected for a while, gives *Vinson* crew members the chance to check the deck and fittings for damage and loose items which could cause foreign object damage (FOD) to an airplane or an engine. Here, immediately forward of the fourth arrester wire, is particularly critical for FOD; after recovery, aircraft sit for a few seconds with their engines at full power, straining against the wire. Under those conditions, jet engines make very efficient vacuum cleaners and can easily "FOD out."

Next page

Sir Arthur Harris, World War II commander of Royal Air Force Bomber Command and a devoted yachtsman, once said that the three least useful things aboard a boat were an umbrella, a wheelbarrow and a Naval Officer. On one the size of the *Vinson,* however, a wheelbarrow can be the best way of delivering practice bombs to the aircraft. Like every piece of nonflying movable equipment on the flight deck, the wheelbarrow is high-visibility yellow; if somebody missed it, and it was behind an aircraft when it started up, the wheelbarrow could be a highly lethal surface-to-surface FOD bomb, capable of knocking out an airplane for the remainder of the cruise.

A crewman checks that the nose-gear towbar on this Grumman A-6 has properly engaged the catapult shuttle. The US Navy has now abandoned the wire bridles that used to attach the airplane to the catapult, in favor of a fixed towbar which is more reliable, reusable and does not convert itself into an antipersonnel weapon if it fails. The hefty nose landing gear link, where the crewman's hand is resting, carries the launch loads into the bomber's airframe.

Next page

Hands raised as if in prayer, the catapult officer guides an F-14 forward before the crew attaches the fighter to the catapult shuttle, the innocuous-seeming little wedge on the deck. Under the catapult officer's feet lie two 300 foot cylinders, each with a metal valve running along its entire length. The shuttle is attached to a piston in each cylinder by a link which opens and closes the valve as it passes, rather like a zipper. As each aircraft moves forward to its launch point, the catapult operator watches steam pressure build up in below-deck accumulators. Even the massive, nuclear-powered *Vinson*, though, must work hard to launch heavy aircraft in rapid sequence in a slack wind, and the catapult operator must be miserly with his pressure.

Seconds before launch, the catapult officer waits for the pilot to complete his final checks on systems and flight controls before giving the catapult operator the signal to fire. The thirty-ton fighter's engines are running at full military power (maximum power without reheat), rotating the aircraft around its mainwheels and causing it to squat at the nose. It is being held in place by the retaining link visible behind the nosewheel. The link is designed to hold the aircraft against full thrust, and to snap off as the catapult reaches its full working pressure. The steel wall behind the aircraft is the jet blast deflector (JBD), which turns the scorching wash from the engines away from the deck. The deck between the aircraft and the JBD has its own internal water-cooling system.

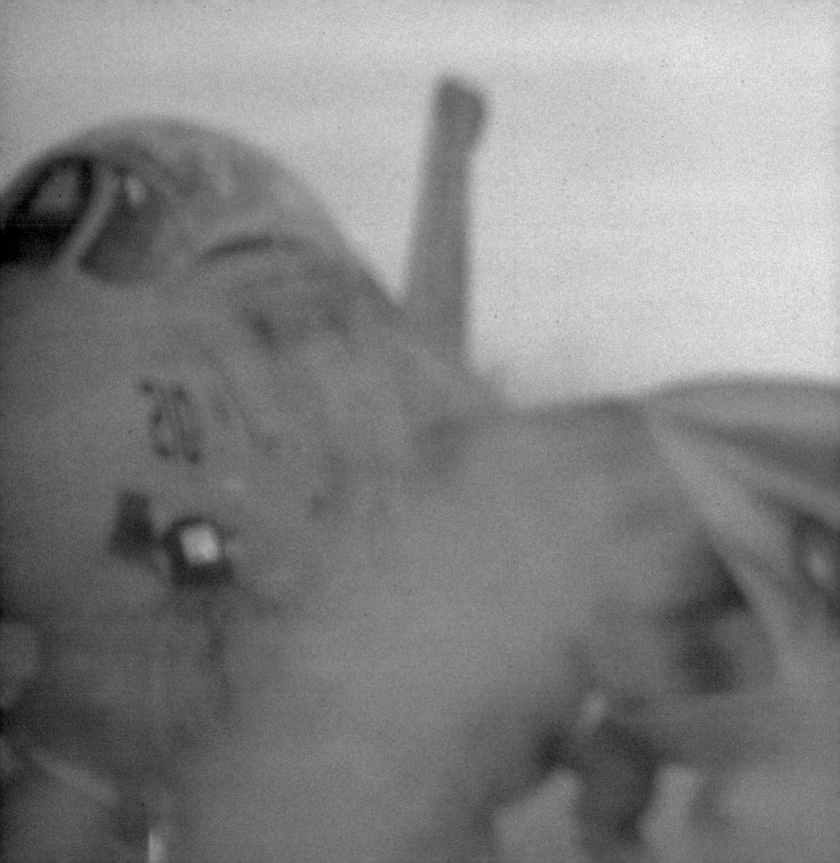

Words are useless in the eardrum-rending
pandemonium of the catapult area, but some
messages are vital. This crewman has just shown
his placard to the pilot, indicating that the catapult
is set for a 64,000 pound airplane: the weight of the
F-14 behind him, plus a few thousand for the wife
and kids. With a thumbs-up from the pilot, he turns
to show it to the catapult operator in his steel-and-
glass foxhole. This is serious; airplanes have been
lost due to incorrectly set catapults, and the crew
has little time to escape if the airplane comes off
the bow without enough energy to fly.

The landing signals officer (LSO) is, at times, the
carrier's hanging judge because, even though
carrier landings are difficult and dangerous, the air
wing cannot afford to lose aircraft in unnecessary
accidents. Invariably an experienced pilot with
many carrier landings behind him, the LSO
watches each landing and awards one of four
grades: ok, which means excellent; fair, which is
not perfect but safe; no grade, which is hazardous;
and cut, which means that your arrival was
definitely unsafe and that you were lucky to make
it aboard in one piece. Too many "no grades," not
to mention "cuts," can qualify a pilot for a desk job.
At night, the LSO can change from hanging judge
to guardian angel, issuing calm, clear instructions
to a rattled pilot on a difficult trap.

Previous page
Here it comes: The big four-blade propellers are churning the air as they fight the holdback bar, the E-2C's crew members are braced back against their seats, the pilot has saluted, and the catapult officer points two fingers down the deck, signaling the operator to fire at any time. Unlike any other take-off in aviation, a carrier launch is not initiated by the pilot. Moreover, the acceleration will outrun the adaptability of the pilot's vestibular system and the airplane's instruments; the key is to trust in procedures until everyone can catch up with the airplane, a few hundred feet off the end of the boat.

The "yellow shirts" who work on the flight deck share some of their concerns with zoo workers who clean out tiger cages—while the tigers are still there. Both ends of an F-14 are deadly at close quarters; the inlets can suck you in, and the exhaust can blow you off the side of the ship, as Tom Wolfe said, "like a candy wrapper." Ear protectors block some but never all of the noise. In fine weather, under an endless California sky, the job is better than it could be but not less forgiving of inattention.

Previous page
End of a good hop: The pilot and radar intercept officer (RIO) of an F-14 walk to debrief after a training mission on a CAVU (ceiling and visibility unlimited) day. The fighter's wings are already folded for deck handling, and it will be towed to the elevator for any maintenance problems or "gripes" to be fixed. Its crew can look forward to routine paperwork. There is no room for bureaucrats aboard a carrier, so administrative chores are divided among the aircrew.

In their element: four F-14s in a practice formation, viewed from the leading aircraft, showing how much visibility aircraft designers provided in the post-Vietnam generation of fighters. Normally, though, the F-14 flies a two-airplane CAP (combat air patrol) formation; a single squadron can keep two CAP stations covered. In that case, the fighters would fly in a less picturesque but more survivable line-abreast formation.

From some angles, the F-14 seems such a jagged hunk of metal that one might wonder if it would fly at all, let alone exceed Mach 2. In flight, though, the bumps and protrusions are less important, and the basically sleek lines are more apparent. F-14 pilots, like virtually all pilots, are confident in their ability to out-shoot and out-dogfight any adversary With a crew of two and the longest standard features list of any air combat fighter, the F-14 is a formidable adversary in any regime.

Pace, practice, perfection

The pace of activity on a carrier's deck is a result of two commanders' conflicting needs. The air wing commander, responsible for his aircraft, can launch only when the ship is steaming into the wind. The carrier's captain, however, is rightly uncomfortable in doing so, because this makes his course easily predictable by an enemy. As a result, launches and recoveries must be compressed into the shortest possible time, and such operations are practiced continually. The comings and goings of the fast tactical jets, meanwhile, are interspersed with the slower, less glamorous but equally vital movements of the air wing's support and early-warning aircraft.

CV-Helo is the official designation of this helicopter's mission, but pilots call it the Angel; one of its tasks is to rescue aircrew if they have to eject close to the carrier. In wartime, the Sikorsky SH-3H has an even more critical mission. Inside its fuselage is a dipping sonar, a device which a hovering helicopter can lower into the water on a sixty-foot cable. The sonar detects and locates submerged submarines, either by listening for their noise or by transmitting sonic "pings" through the water. The carrier captain's nightmare is the silent submarine which moves into ambush ahead of the task force, lets the escorts run over it and then attacks the carrier with short-range missiles. The CV-Helo, with dipping sonar and homing torpedoes, represents the inner ring of the carrier's defenses.

Somewhere among the top ten winners of the aeronautical Ugly Contest is the Boeing Vertol CH-46 Sea Knight, known to its operators as the Phrog because of its bulbous cockpit glass and tail-down posture. Most Phrogs are used as Marine Corps assault transports, but the Navy uses the type for the specialized task of VERTREP (vertical replenishment). Munitions and spares, up to and including complete engines, are the priority Phrog loads, but "luxury goods" such as perishable foods and recent movies can also make the manifest. Return loads include components which cannot be repaired aboard the ship.

Next page

Sometimes, as here, the Phrog acts as a flying crane, lifting supply pallets across the gap between the *Vinson* and a replenishment ship while the carrier takes on jet fuel through a hose. Supplies can be lifted over longer distances. Advantages of the tandem-twin layout, a Boeing Vertol trademark since the 1950s, include the fact that the total rotor area is large, and the downwash is accordingly gentle. This type of helicopter is also easier to hold straight and level when hovering or—as in many VERTREP missions—keeping station over a moving ship.

An Angel is airborne during every launch and recovery; the F-14 here is ready to go from the *Vinson*'s inner waist catapult as soon as the SH-3H is a safe distance away. A maximum-rate launch is about to start; in the background, beyond the parked aircraft, the JBD is raised behind an A-6 on the port bow catapult. Noise and organized chaos will reign in seconds, and anybody who does not know exactly what he is doing will be better off somewhere else.

Next page

Looking very futuristic from this angle, one of *Vinson*'s four Grumman E-2C Hawkeyes catches a wire. Nicknamed Hummer, the E-2C is critical to the fleet because there is nothing else that can even do part of its job. The Hummer is a flying radar station, carrying more than six tons of electronic equipment; the disk-shaped "rotodome" above its back houses an antenna array for the APS-125 radar, and rotates in flight to scan a full circle around the aircraft. The three radar operators sit facing sideways at a row of consoles toward the rear of the fuselage, the electronics occupying the front of the cabin. Cruising at 24,000 feet, Hawkeye's radar can track other aircraft up to 200 nautical miles away. It can also track low-flying targets and surface ships, which the curvature of the earth conceals from shipboard radar. The best-equipped ship is blind to such threats without an airborne radar, and the loss of HMS *Sheffield* in the Falklands showed how dangerous that blindness can be. The Israel Defense Force-Air Force has used the E-2C very successfully, in some cases tracking Syrian fighters as soon as they left their runways.

An E-2C is a few seconds from launch as an F-14 approaches for recovery and two more F-14s pass abeam the ship. The E-2C and F-14 work as a team, with the Hawkeye detecting targets at maximum range and vectoring the fighters toward the target. The fighters can avoid using their own radars (and betraying their position and intentions) until they are close enough to identify and engage the target. Neither the E-2C nor its radar is new, but they have been continuously updated to improve performance and reliability. New E-2Cs have a passive detection system (PDS), to detect and identify air and surface targets by their surface emissions, and a new radar antenna which improves the system's resistance to jamming. The E-2Cs may also receive more powerful and more efficient engines, so that they can remain on station longer at higher altitudes, improving their ability to detect low-level targets at long distance.

Next page
The Hummer's peculiar shape is the result of putting a long-range radar into an aircraft that will have a useful performance and leave room for other airplanes aboard the carrier. The long-span wings are for efficient cruising at high altitude, and the ailerons droop with the flaps to reduce the landing speed; the wings twist and fold back for stowage, and the rotodome is lowered hydraulically. The designers did not want the vertical fins to obstruct the radar signals, but needed a lot of fin area in case the Hummer had to land with one of its 4,900 horsepower Allison T56 turboprops inoperative. So they ended up with four fins, three of them carrying tandem-hinged rudders. For the same reason—avoiding interference with radar—Hamilton Standard developed special propellers for the Hawkeye, the first to have fiberglass skins over a foam core on a solid aluminum spar.

First cousin to the Hummer is the Grumman C-2A carrier-onboard-delivery (COD) transport. First flown in 1964, the C-2A has the wings, engines, landing gear and tail of the E-2, but its portly fuselage and rear loading ramp accommodate anything and anybody which urgently needs to be on the carrier or off it when the carrier is at sea and outside helicopter range of land—from critical spares to the sick or badly injured. The C-2A has a range of 1,000 nautical miles with a 10,000 pound payload or twenty-eight passengers. Its official name is Greyhound, which in view of its ice-cream-and-french-fries-diet proportions must have been somebody's idea of a joke.

Two fingers outstretched, the catapult officer signals the operator to launch a C-2. Fighting the holdback at full power, the propellers generate powerful tip vortices, visible as spiral contrails in the late-afternoon light. C-2As are not based aboard the carriers, but operate from shore bases around the world and, on assignment, stage through the nearest airport to the carrier's predicted position. For this reason, a C-2 can turn up almost anywhere. Other attractions of C-2 duty include the fact that this airplane's crew will be enjoying the cultural attractions of San Diego in two hours or so, while the *Vinson* continues its cruise.

Next page

The *Vinson*'s deck crew prepare for a series of evening recoveries, with two SH-3H Angels warming up for launch and the landing deck cleared. This time of day presents its own operational challenges, particularly if—as here—the wind direction requires the carrier to steam into the brightly lit eastern sky. The C-2 in the foreground will depart before the *Vinson*'s own aircraft return.

"Ship shape and *Vinson* fashion"

Carriers are controversial, boosted under one administration and cut down in the next. Building a carrier costs $2.5 billion. The cost of the aircraft on board and reserves on shore adds an equal amount. The carrier itself has only limited protection against air or submarine attack, so it is accompanied by escort ships; the total task force, or battle group, can cost $17 billion. Operating costs are stupendous; 5,000 men aboard the carrier alone. Questions of utility and vulnerability loom large, but the Navy remains confident that it can carry out its offensive missions.

All four of the *Vinson*'s catapults are visible in this wide-angle shot. The rate at which a carrier can launch aircraft is as important as the number of aircraft it can carry. If a large airstrike is being dispatched, the first aircraft to go must wait for the last aircraft launched to reach their proper stations, and as a result the time between the first and last take-off must be deducted from the formation's flight endurance and range. Hence the four catapults: The two widely spaced bow catapults can be used almost simultaneously, and an aircraft can warm up on one waist catapult while another is launched. Nominally, *Vinson* can launch an aircraft every thirty seconds.

USS *Carl Vinson*, like all the US Navy's supercarriers, is an evolutionary design based on the first of the class, USS *Forrestal.* The ships were originally designated CVA (carrier, heavier-than-air, attack), and were intended to launch nuclear-armed strategic bombers. After that mission was assumed by the Polaris submarine-launched missile system, the ships became CV multipurpose carriers, and antisubmarine warfare aircraft occupied the space formerly taken up by the bombers. There are now twelve supercarriers in the US Navy, together with the older and smaller *Midway* and *Coral Sea.* Ten of the supercarriers were built in the 1950s and early 1960s; USS *Nimitz* was launched in 1972, *Vinson* was commissioned in 1982, and three more are being built.

Not even *Carl Vinson* looks big from the pilot's vantage point. The aim is to catch the third arrester wire—the four wires are visible, where the impact of many landings has worn away the centerline stripe—and the wire is a small target in daytime. Add night and foul weather, and it is possible to have some idea of the task facing naval pilots. Some research has indicated that carrier pilots are under more stress during night landings than they experience in combat. Clearly visible at the stern are the two of *Vinson*'s four eight-round launchers for RIM-7 Sea Sparrow surface-to-air missiles (SAMs, the rectangular boxes at either edge of the flight deck). Below them, characteristic white thimble radomes surmount two of the ship's Phalanx defensive guns. Phalanx is a fully automatic close-in weapon system (CIWS) based on a six-barrel Gatling-type twenty-millimeter cannon. It is a last-ditch defense against incoming cruise missiles, and simply hosepipes one hundred shells per second toward the missile's predicted track, aiming to chew off enough of its airframe to put it off course in the last few hundred yards of its flight. US Navy philosophy is to avoid mounting long-range SAMs aboard the carrier, but instead to rely on a layered defense including F-14s and the Standard missiles carried by escort ships. The opening, or fantail, in the carrier's stern is used for testing aircraft engines.

The characteristic shape of an aircraft carrier deck
dates back to the 1950s, and was invented in
Britain to cater to fast jet aircraft, with their high
landing speeds. The basic change then made by
the British was to slant the landing strip relative to
the axis of the ship, extending it on a sponson, so
that both ends of the landing strip are unobstructed
even when aircraft are on deck. An aircraft that
misses the arrester wires (called boltering) near
the stern, has enough runway left to accelerate
back to flying speed and take off again. Meanwhile,
the entire deck starboard and forward of the
recovery area is available for aircraft parking and
launching, so that an angled-deck carrier can
launch and recover aircraft at the same time.
However, the Air Boss' objective is to handle
aircraft as rapidly as possible, in order to
concentrate the carrier's air strength and reduce to
a minimum the time it spends steaming in a
straight line into wind. This is best accomplished
by cyclic operations, in which the deck and deck
crew are alternately organized for maximum
launch rate and maximum recovery rate. The
advantage of the angled deck in this case is that it
provides space for two more catapults at the front
of the landing area. Here, one of these has just
launched an EA-6B Prowler, and a second Prowler
is ready to go on the second waist catapult. An S-3
Viking is ready for launch from the starboard bow
catapult.

Previous page

The carrier's "island" has been a near-standard feature of the class since its very early days. Originally, its function was to house the funnels and conduct smoke up and away from the deck. A nuclear-powered ship has no funnels, but the ship still needs a place for radar and other sensors, and a high-level visual lookout is still important. Here, observers in Pri-Fly watch an A-6E complete a successful recovery. The wire can be seen fully stretched behind the aircraft, indicating that its engines are still developing full military power. Standard procedure in every carrier landing is to open the throttles as soon as the wheels hit the deck, in case the aircraft bolters; if the pilot applied power only when he knew he had boltered, he would be too late and the airplane would sink into the water. The only thing you assume in the Navy is the worst possible case.

"Bewildering" is a small word for the array of antennae that festoon the *Vinson's* island like sea life to a submerged crag. Directly above the bridge, visible in side view, is the antenna for the ship's main air surveillance radar. The antenna outrigged from the rear of the mainmast is a tracking and illuminating antenna for the Sea Sparrow missile system; Sea Sparrow is semiactive, homing in on radar energy transmitted by the ship and reflected by the target. The rearmost radar antenna is mainly used for air traffic control in the vicinity of the ship. Other systems visible here include the SLQ-17 electronic warfare system, which intercepts and classifies electronic signals related to cruise missiles and missile platforms such as ships or bombers, and retransmits false echo signals which cause the launcher's radars to give inaccurate range and bearing information to the radar.

Deck equipment includes tractors and a large mobile crane, which may be needed if an aircraft crash-lands and cannot be moved by other means. A blocked recovery zone cannot be tolerated by a carrier; unlike a land base, it has no second runway, and much of the time there is no alternative landing field within range. In normal operations, US Navy aircraft are bombed-up on the open deck; carriers can survive (and have) weapon explosions on deck, but a detonation on the hangar deck could be devastating.

Next page
The flat plate of the surveillance radar antenna is clearly visible here; it is described as a 3-D radar because it can accurately measure a target's altitude as well as its range and bearing. The range of the radar is limited by little more than the horizon, but it cannot see beyond it, and a low-flying aircraft may be invisible to radar but only two minutes from the carrier. Moreover, it betrays the precise bearing of the carrier to an attacker such as a Backfire, which carries its own sensitive listening devices. This is why the Hawkeye is an essential part of the carrier's complement. US Navy carrier groups regularly practice EMCON exercises in waters which are known to be patrolled by Soviet forces, carefully monitoring Soviet radio traffic for signs that their ships have been detected.

Previous page
No carrier can match the steely grace of a well-designed cruiser, because the need for a deep hangar, high above the waterline, and a massive flat deck above the hangar, conflict with the need for a slim, high-speed hull. The resulting shape is inevitably a compromise, and is further marred by additions, such as the forward Sea Sparrow sponsons visible here.

The size of a carrier is a function of several factors. One starting point is the size and complexity of the aircraft which a carrier must field in order to survive and be effective; in a world of radar-guided cruise missiles and SAM-defended targets, all-weather fighters and strike aircraft are essential, and these are bigger and need more maintenance than older, simpler types. The carrier must have space to store these aircraft and catapult capacity to launch them at a reasonable rate. There must also be space for weapons and fuel: A carrier's two strike squadrons alone can, in theory, deliver almost 1,000 tons of bombs in three days of missions, burn an equivalent quantity of aviation fuel and jettison hundreds of light but bulky drop tanks. Fighters may expend less ordnance, but their missiles are bulky in relation to their weight. And then there is the crew: *Forrestal* was originally designed to accommodate 3,800 men, but maintenance-hungry modern aircraft and weapons have driven the complement close to 5,800 for the *Vinson* and the others of its class. Attempts to downsize the US aircraft carrier have met with little success; a somewhat smaller carrier could perform a useful mission, but the question is whether the expense of a complete class redesign would be justified.

An F-14 leaves the *Vinson*'s starboard bow catapult, its size signifying the importance of the fleet air defense mission to the carrier. Three other elements of the carrier's defenses are visible here. The forward, starboard Sea Sparrow launcher is visible on its sponson, which it shares with a Phalanx gun. (The Navy studies which led to Phalanx started after the Israeli destroyer *Eilat* was sunk by an SS-N-3 Styx cruise missile in 1967, and the system became operational in the late 1970s.) The barbel-like antennae projecting from the ship's side are part of its electronic warfare system.

A-6s, Prowlers and F-14s line the deck in the half-light; the single-seat A-7s are tucked away below, and the night belongs to the big two-seaters. The lights that illuminate the deck are designed to be as inconspicuous as possible away from the ship, but once again there is an essential compromise between reducing visibility and being able to operate safely.

Next page
Dawn breaks, and the carrier group's primary long-range defenses are ready to launch; the F-14s will seek the enemy in the sky, and the S-3 will hunt him beneath the water.

Constant action for the carrier's air wing

No simulator can come close to reproducing carrier operations. The only way to make carrier flying acceptably safe is continuous training, until launches, traps and night refueling become second nature. The carrier's air wing is in constant action as long as the ship is cruising. Another difference between a carrier and a normal airbase is that it can never count on reinforcements, and is usually on its own. What it has on board is what it will go to war with, both in terms of the total number of aircraft and the mix of types. As a result, carriers always have a variety of aircraft of different types and ages aboard, while a land-based unit is normally equipped with aircraft of the same type from the same production block. A balance must be struck between fighters and attack aircraft, and between quantity and capability; if the carrier has only the most capable and complex aircraft, the air wing

will not be able to maintain high sortie rates. In early 1986, *Vinson* embarked two twelve-aircraft squadrons of F-14s, two squadrons of A-7s and a single heavy attack squadron with A-6 Intruders.

Vought's A-7E is officially named the Corsair II, but since Vietnam its pilots have called it the SLUF, or Short Little Ugly (. . . er, umm, let's see . . .) Fella. It was designed in 1963 as a clear-weather attack aircraft to replace the A-4 Skyhawk, with much greater range and better avionics to improve navigation and bombing accuracy. The design started life as a development of Vought's F-8 Crusader fighter, and the basic layout is similar, but the A-7 is completely different in every detail. Its ability to carry a heavy warload over a long distance is still matched by very few aircraft of its size, thanks to a big, thick wing (which allows it to lift heavy loads), a great deal of internal fuel capacity and an efficient turbofan engine without a fuel-thirsty afterburner.

A SLUF driver completes his last checks before launch. The A-7E, now the standard Navy version of the type, was introduced in 1970 and was based on the USAF's A-7D. The E-model was the first US Navy aircraft to carry an internally mounted General Electric M61A1 six-barrel Gatling gun; the muzzle is visible above the nosewheel. Other features introduced with the A-7E included a more powerful and more efficient engine, Allison TF41 (a development of the British Rolls-Royce Spey, built under license); a head-up display, also British-developed; and many avionics improvements.

The A-7E has six underwing weapon pylons, four stressed to carry 3,500 pounds each and two rated at 2,500 pounds. The A-7 also has launch rails for AIM-9L Sidewinder missiles on the sides of the fuselage, giving it a very useful self-defense capability without occupying one of the six main weapon stations. That gives the SLUF a theoretical maximum weapon load of 20,000 pounds, equal to its empty weight. While such loads are rarely carried in service, the ability to trade external weapons for drop tanks can further extend the type's range. The girth of the fuselage, accommodating the internal fuel load, is very apparent from this angle.

Next page

The A-7E's nose radome contains a Texas Instruments APQ-126 forward-looking radar, which warns the pilot of terrain in cloud and provides a radar map of the target area. It can also be fitted with a forward-looking infra-red (FLIR) system—a video camera which responds to heat energy rather than light—in a pod on the inner starboard pylon. The FLIR projects a picture of the scene ahead on the pilot's head-up display, even at night or in haze. The A-7E can also act as a very effective tanker: This aircraft has a "buddy store" under its port outer pylon, containing an inflight refueling hose and drogue, and a reel mechanism driven by the small turbine on the nose of the pod. By 1992, the SLUF is due to be replaced by the McDonnell Douglas F-18 Hornet, which is not only an effective light attack aircraft but an excellent fighter as well. However, the Navy's A-7Es will have plenty of airframe life left, and could still be reworked into low-cost bombers for export customers.

When the supercarriers adopted their multipurpose role in the late 1960s, the US Navy began to retire its specialized antisubmarine carriers and started development of a new antisubmarine warfare (ASW) aircraft for the supercarriers. This aircraft, the Lockheed S-3A Viking, made its first flight in 1972 and entered service in 1974. Nicknamed Hoover, because of the characteristic noise of its high-bypass-ratio General Electric TF34 turbofan engines, the short-coupled S-3 is designed to patrol for several hours, around and ahead of the fleet. The rear fuselage contains launching tubes for sonobuoys (expendable devices, with a life of a few hours, which send out sound waves through the water, listen for echoes and relay data back to the aircraft by radio). Cruising at 30,000 feet, the S-3 can sow and monitor sonobuoys over more than 10,000 square miles of ocean. The aircraft carries a specialized acoustic signal processor, with two operators, which localizes the sonobuoys and analyzes and compares their signals to locate submerged submarines and identify them by their characteristic sounds. When a target is detected, the S-3 dives rapidly to a lower altitude, pinpoints the submarine with a MAD (magnetic anomaly detector) sensor in its retractable tailboom, and attacks with a nuclear depth bomb or an Mk46 homing torpedo. Additionally, the S-3 carries radar and passive electronic sensors to detect surface targets.

Some idea of the size of the ASW problem and the S-3's maintenance needs is given by the fact that *Vinson* carries ten Hoovers in order to maintain coverage around the ship. The aircraft is very densely packed with avionics defined in the late 1960s, and its heavy demands on the carrier have been a problem since the ASW role was assigned to the supercarriers. An improved S-3B version has been developed, but is not likely to be bought in large numbers. Instead, the Navy plans to develop an ASW version of the V-22 Osprey tilt-rotor aircraft, resolving a number of significant problems. The Osprey can take off like a helicopter, so the carrier need not turn into wind to launch and recover it—the fact that ASW operations do not fit into normal strike or CAP cycle times has been a problem. Also, it can refuel from almost any escort ship (by ship-to-air refueling if necessary), and because it can hover it can use a more sensitive, more accurate dipping sonar for its final location and attack run. Ultimately, ASW could be moved back off the aircraft carrier to a smaller ship, making room for another heavy attack squadron.

The primary strike weapon of the *Vinson*'s air wing is the Grumman A-6E Intruder, designed in 1957 to meet a Navy requirement for a long-range attack bomber that would be capable of hitting mobile or imprecisely located land targets in bad weather. The first aircraft flew in 1960, and the type entered service in 1963. The much improved A-6E became operational in December 1972 and is now the standard service version of the type. The Intruder's distinctive shape is largely a result of the all-weather requirement, which at the time dictated the use of a large radar antenna in a large-diameter radome. In fact, the first Intruders had two radar systems, one for navigation and one for search-and-track. The crew of two sit side-by-side, so that both are in a position to watch out for obstacles in low-level flight, and sit high enough to afford a good view over the nose. As a result, the forward fuselage is bulky; the body tapers sharply aft of the cockpit to reduce drag at high speed, giving the Intruder a somewhat tadpole-like appearance. The Intruder is subsonic because no supersonic aircraft could carry out its mission and land on a carrier, at the time it was developed. And the broad swept wing is optimized for load-carrying and efficiency at high subsonic speeds. The A-6E is to be followed by the A-6F, with a new radar, improved cockpit and other changes, which will sustain the force until the ultimate replacement, the Stealth strike bomber called the ATA (advanced tactical aircraft), enters service in the mid-1990s.

The A-6E carries 2,500 pounds of electronics. The primary sensor is Norden Systems' APQ-148 radar, a Ku-band system, operating at higher frequency than X-band fighter radars. This gives it higher resolution and greater accuracy, essential for use against ground targets. The radar also has AMTI (airborne moving target identification) circuitry, enabling it to distinguish objects from the ground clutter, moving above a certain threshold speed. Not only does it provide the bombardier/navigator (BN) with a radar display, but it also provides many inputs for the pilot's vertical display indicator, a CRT (cathode ray tube) display which long foreshadowed the "glass cockpits" of modern commercial and military aircraft. The A-6F will have a new-generation, improved Norden radar, capable of identifying a ship as much as eighty miles away, and new cockpit displays.

The dual flat windshields of the A-6 provide the pilot and BN with an excellent view, even in rain, but give the aircraft a somewhat surprised expression. The engine installation is also unusual, but dates back to the advent of the Polaris missile. When the Navy saw that the missile would replace its carrier-based strategic bombers, it planned a new generation of much smaller carriers, and specified that the Grumman bomber's jet nozzles should swivel downward to reduce its landing and take-off speeds to fit the projected ships. The ships were never built, and only the prototypes had such nozzles, but the engine location, chosen because the nozzles had to be near the center of gravity, was the small carriers' legacy to the A-6.

Next page
Flaps and leading-edge slats extend across the full span of the A-6E wing; the aircraft is controlled in roll by flaperons or spoilers on the upper surface of the wing, ahead of the flaps. Powerplants are unreheated turbojets, Pratt & Whitney J52s developing 9,300 pounds of thrust each. In the new A-6F, they will be replaced by General Electric F404s, newer engines which are more powerful, more reliable and more efficient and are also fitted to the F-18. In another development program, Boeing is designing a new wing for the A-6 in light, high-strength graphite/epoxy composite material. Note the row of holes in the fuselage side, behind the wings; they are launch tubes for decoys to deceive missiles. The decoys include chaff (metalized fiberglass strands, which produce a massive echo on radar) and flares to seduce heat-seeking missiles away from their targets.

Previous page

The A-6E can launch at a maximum gross weight of 58,600 pounds and carry twelve 565-pound Mk82 bombs to a target 775 nautical miles away, covering the last hundred miles to the target on the deck. In a less-discussed mission, it can launch with two B43 nuclear weapons and three 300 gallon drop tanks, and hit a target 880 nautical miles from the carrier group. The Intruder also carries antiradar missiles such as the AGM-45 Shrike and the new AGM-88 HARM (high-speed antiradiation missile) which home in on hostile radar emitters and either destroy them or force them to shut down. The new A-6F will be able to carry the AIM-120 advanced medium-range air-to-air missile (AMRAAM) and, later, the long-range advanced air-to-air missile (AAAM), and will be able to back up the F-14 for long-range air defense.

The menacing EA-6B Prowler is a radical and highly specialized development of the Intruder. The US Navy has long recognized the importance of electronic warfare (EW) in military aviation, and in late 1966 the service started development of the world's first dedicated tactical EW aircraft. The Prowler's forward fuselage is stretched to accommodate a second cockpit for two EW operators, and the rear fuselage is extended to balance the aircraft. Instead of radar, navigational/attack electronics and weapons, the Prowler carries four tons of EW gear, internally and in up to five pods under the wings and centerline, which constitute the Eaton-AIL ALQ-99 countermeasures system (this particular aircraft carries only three pods). The pods have their own generators, driven by turbines on the nose of the pod, to reduce the load on the aircraft's electrical generating system. In the basic ALQ-99 system, each pod is designed to jam a specific waveband, but the new ICAP-2 (increased capability) version has pods which can jam in any two of seven wavebands.

Two Prowlers await launch from the waist catapults. The ALQ-99 is designed to intercept hostile radar transmissions, with the antenna at the tip of the fin, and jam them by radiating high-power signals at the same frequency toward the source antenna. Even if the antenna is not pointing directly toward the EA-6B, the jamming signal can still enter through its sidelobes. The signal appears as intense radial streaks on the enemy operator's radar scope, making it impossible to track targets except in a small clear zone close to the radar. Grumman has claimed that jamming can reduce radar range by a factor of 20. The power of the system is so great that engineers worried that radiation from the pods might be harmful to the crew, so a gold film, so thin as to be effectively transparent, was applied to the cockpit canopy to exclude electromagnetic radiation. In fact, there was no health hazard, but the canopies remain in service and their gold tone is visible here.

Two features of the A-6 are visible here: the split wingtip speedbrakes and, under the nose, the ball turret which houses the TRAM (target recognition and attack, multisensor) system. First delivered in 1978, and now being retrofitted to all A-6Es in the fleet, TRAM is a highly sophisticated and capable set of sensors which complement the APQ-148 radar. The radar is used to detect targets at long range and points a long-focus FLIR in the TRAM turret on to the target, giving the BN a TV-quality picture of the objective at night or, to some extent, in haze. This makes it possible to classify land targets, or to positively identify a ship. To improve tracking and reduce workload, an automatic tracker is being added to the TRAM system. TRAM also incorporates a laser designator and laser tracker, which can be used to mark a target for a laser-guided bomb or missile. "Buddy" designation, when one aircraft designates the target from a distance while another closes to release range, launches the weapon and immediately escapes, can also be used. It can also be used if the tactical situation demands it. The laser tracker aboard the "shooter" will automatically direct the BN's attention and the FLIR toward the designation spot from the illuminating aircraft. TRAM will be used in conjunction with the Navy's new rocket-propelled Skipper stand-off bomb. The A-6E takes a great deal of maintenance, some fifty manhours' worth for every hour it flies. But how many complex, 1960s-technology computer systems end every working day with an impact equivalent to being pushed off a loading dock?

There are two prime threats to the survival of the carrier battle group. One of them is the submarine. S-3s, land-based P-3s and, above all, the sonar equipment of the carrier's escorts provide a dense defensive thicket around the carrier, and the chances that a submarine could penetrate the thicket and execute a successful attack are acceptable. But the escorts' weapons are of little use against the other prime threat, the long-range, missile-launching aircraft. The Soviet Navy has developed this class of weapon since the 1950s, and by 1961 was testing an eight-ton air-launched, rocket-powered cruise missile, known to NATO as the AS-4 Kitchen. Its size and shape left US naval analysts in no doubt that it had, essentially, one mission: to be fired outside the range of shipboard SAMs, break through the defenses by sheer speed, home in on the carrier with its own radar and sink or cripple it with a massive hollow-charge warhead. The Tupolev Backfire bomber, of which almost 300 are in service, can haul three of these weapons into the air. Shooting down the missiles is possible but offers poor chances of success. The answer is to shoot down the bombers before they can launch their weapons, and the only system in the carrier group which can do that is the Grumman F-14A Tomcat swing-wing, long-range fighter.

Previous page

With the possible exception of the Soviet's Mikoyan MiG-31 Foxhound, the F-14A is the world's most comprehensively equipped fighter. The chin housing which is attracting the attention of the deck crewman here accommodates an ECM antenna in the lower section; above it, in a cylindrical casing, is a unique device called the Northrop AXX-1 Television Camera Set (TCS). The TCS is a stabilized, telephoto video camera, steered by the radar, which presents a clear, magnified image of any target on a video screen in the rear cockpit. With the TCS, targets can be positively identified at ranges in excess of ten miles. When rules of engagement require positive visual identification before opening fire, as is often the case, the TCS can be vital.

Visible under the belly of this F-14 is the Tomcat's primary weapon: the Hughes AIM-54 Phoenix air-to-air missile (AAM). Very sophisticated and very expensive—more than $1 million per round—Phoenix was the first AAM in service to carry its own radar system to illuminate and home in on its target, and is described as an "active-radar" AAM. Most medium-range missiles are semiactive, and home in on radar energy transmitted by the launch belly of this F-14 is the Tomcat's primary weapon: the Hughes AIM-54 Phoenix air-to-air missile (AAM). Very sophisticated and very expensive— more than $1 million per round—Phoenix was the first AAM in service to carry its own radar system to illuminate and home in on its target, and is described as an "active-radar" AAM. Most medium-range missiles are semiactive, and home in on radar energy transmitted by the launch aircraft and reflected by the target. The drawback

is that the launch aircraft must keep its radar fixed on the target until the missile hits, so that it can only engage one target at a time. In theory, though, an F-14 can have six Phoenix missiles in the air at once, each aimed at a different target. After launch, the missile steers toward its predicted impact point using its own inertial navigation system. If the target changes course, the aircraft sends corrected steering commands to the missile via a datalink until the weapon's active radar locks on. Under ideal conditions—against a conspicuous, high-flying, unmaneuverable target like a Backfire—the Mach 5 Phoenix has a launch range of more than 100 nautical miles, and the F-14 may still be as much as 70 nautical miles from the target when the missile hits it. The only fighter with a comparable missile is, once again, the MiG-31; the Soviet fighter's AA-9 Amos missile is almost identical to Phoenix.

Years of exposure to F-15s and F-16s have made the F-14 seem almost normal now, but it looked like something from outer space when Grumman unveiled the mock-up in 1969. All the features have a purpose; the humped forward fuselage improves the view for the crew, while the twin vertical fins sustain directional control at high angles of attack, when a single fin would be useless in the dead air behind the broad fuselage. The engines are widely separated, so that even a severe hit is unlikely to put both of them out of action, and fuel is carried in the fuselage between the engines, rather than above them, so that ruptured tanks do not drain into the engine bays.

Next page

The F-14 was the first fighter to be designed in the light of combat reports from Vietnam, which showed that agility and good pilot visibility—which had been deliberately sacrificed to straight-line performance and weapon load in the 1950s—were still critically important. As a result, the Grumman fighter emerged with a big, thin-framed canopy, giving the crew an excellent view in all directions, and a built-in M61A1 Gatling cannon. Herein lies the big difference between the MiG-31 and the F-14; the Soviet fighter is strictly a straight-line airplane, and would be kitty chow in close combat.

Previous page
The nose of the F-14A houses the Hughes AWG-9 radar and fire-control system. It is a pulse-Doppler radar; that is to say, each returning pulse of radar energy is analyzed in terms of Doppler shifts, the phenomenon that makes the noise of a speeding car seem to rise and fall in pitch as it passes the listener. Exploiting this phenomenon, the AWG-9 radar can pick out and track low-flying aircraft against ground or sea clutter, because their echoes have a different Doppler characteristic. The AWG-9 was the first radar to combine this technique with ''track-while-scan'' operation, in which the radar searches the sky for new targets while continuing to display the tracks of several targets already discovered. Previous fighter radars could track targets only by locking onto them and ignoring all others.

An F-14 lines up to engage the catapult shuttle. The strakes on the upper surface of the wing stiffen the light fairings above the roots of the variable geometry (VG) wings. Also called variable wing sweep, it was a popular design feature in the early 1960s, but was losing some of its reputation by the time the F-14 appeared. However, the Grumman designers had good reasons for choosing such a layout in this case.

Previous page
The F-14 is the only true second-generation VG type in service, having drawn extensively on experience with the F-111, which Grumman helped to build. Compared with other VG designs, the wing loses relatively little area as it retracts, and the relationship of the wing and tailplane is different from that on the F-111 or the Soviet MiG-23, both of which have the maneuverability of a freight train. The F-14 also has automatic sweep control to optimize wing sweep for different combat conditions, and can be flown out to very low airspeed and high angles of attack. At supersonic speeds, two small vanes pop out of the fixed wing glove to reduce drag and improve maneuverability.

The great span of the F-14's spread wings make it much safer in recovery than previous high-performance fighters. While the F-4 trapped at 140 knots, the F-14 typically approaches the ramp at 130 knots or less, and handles far better at such speeds. Long span also translates into high efficiency in cruising flight, an essential feature for the CAP mission. The F-14 can remain on station for an hour, 300 nautical miles from the carrier, carrying a 5,000 pound load of missiles.

Flaps extend across the full span of the F-14's wing, and the fighter is controlled in roll by over-wing spoilers and by differential movements of its large horizontal stabilizers. The aircraft is also quite short-coupled, with a short tail arm in relation to its wing area, and the result is that the stabilizers move rapidly over a wide angle at low speeds. The fighter's wingspread, its short tail, and the rather dramatic deflections of its stabilizers have earned it the affectionate nickname Turkey among carrier crews.

Previous page
An F-14 leaves one of the *Vinson*'s waist catapults.
The F-14A uses afterburner for take-off; the
greater thrust of the F110 engine will make it
possible for the F-14A Plus and F-14D to launch
on military power, saving an enormous amount of
fuel and increasing the fighter's range and
endurance.

The Tomcat has been in service since 1974; this
example seems to have seen a lot of use, and
includes a new canopy. Like many other Tomcats,
it has not yet been fitted with the TCS, and instead
has a streamlined fairing over the nose pod. Older
F-14As will be allocated to the Navy Reserve as
the F-14A Plus and F-14D become available.

Grumman's designers avoided the structural and aerodynamic complications of putting swiveling weapon pylons on the outer wings, and instead provided the F-14 with stores stations under the fuselage, the engine nacelles and the fixed inner wing sections, or "gloves." This aircraft is carrying the removable ventral pallet which can accommodate four Phoenix AAMs. Without the pallet, four AIM-7 Sparrow semiactive medium-range AAMs can be carried in troughs under the fuselage, the rearmost trough being visible just ahead of the arrester hook. Sparrow is the weapon of choice for escort missions, when maneuvering targets may be encountered. The pylon under the glove, kinked outward to clear the landing gear, can carry a Phoenix, although a Sparrow and a Sidewinder are more usually carried. The F-14D should be able to carry two of the new AMRAAM missiles, with the same multiple-shot capability as Phoenix, on each glove pylon. A pair of 300 gallon auxiliary fuel tanks can be carried under the nacelles.

Previous page
Swing wings usually exact a price from the designer in weight and complexity, which is why most modern fighters do not have them. For a carrier-based fighter, however, the penalty is smaller because the wings have to fold anyway. The F-14's wings have an "oversweep" position, seven degrees more than the maximum inflight sweep, for carrier stowage. Note the small rounded lump or discus where the leading edge of the movable wing meets the fixed glove; the discus seals and fairs the gap between the two as the wings move on their pivots. The wing pivots are set well outboard, and are joined by a massive eighteen-foot box girder made of machined titanium panels welded together by electron beams. The pivot pins and wing box carry the entire flight loads as the F-14, which may weigh over 40,000 pounds ready for combat, pulls maneuvers which may subject its airframe to nine times the force of gravity.

Combat air patrol continues around the clock when the carrier is on alert. The appearance of the AS-4 missile, with its active-radar terminal homing system, ushered in an era when carriers could be successfully attacked from the air regardless of light or weather conditions. The answer to the threat, the F-14, may be expensive in money, carrier space and manpower, but there is no alternative in sight.

The F-14 itself will outlive all its contemporaries as a first-rank fighter aircraft. The F-14D is expected to be in production throughout most of the 1990s, and it will be at least the year 2000 before a replacement begins to enter Navy service. In 1987, that replacement was expected to be a carrier-based version of the Air Force's Advanced Tactical Fighter, either the Lockheed F-22 or Northrop F-23. Under a joint-service agreement, both are being designed so that they can be modified for shipboard use.

The Navy sees no end to the carriers themselves. The big ships show no signs of wearing out. Operational and financial reality exclude any possibility that they will be replaced by bigger and more powerful ships, as previous carriers were. Unlike cruisers or destroyers, which are designed around their armament and their command and intelligence suites, carriers are very big, very fast and specialized transport vessels, which can be refitted with new aircraft, new support equipment and new electronics for a fraction of the cost of a new boat, even a smaller one.

The argument over the effectiveness and affordability of the carrier will continue. Critics charge, quite correctly, that much of the cost of building and operating the carrier, its air wing and its escorts is spent on protecting the carrier itself from destruction or crippling damage, and assert that a situation in which a single, nonnuclear missile hit could defeat an entire task force is untenable. The Navy has always challenged the critics to propose a better way of doing what the supercarriers do, in many situations short of Backfire-versus-Tomcat total war. The *Vinson* and the other big boats provide the United States with a dozen airbases which can be located within strike range of ninety percent of the world's land mass, which are immune to artillery, terrorism and most other conventional forms of attack, and can be used without asking permission of other nations. The mere presence of a pair of carrier groups can reverse the military balance in many parts of the world. Gunboat diplomacy, yes; but it was not international pressure which removed Argentine forces from the Falklands and, ultimately, put a military junta on trial for many murders before a democratic government's jury. It was a military task force, its mission dependent on the survival of one ship: an aircraft carrier.